Ushering With A Mission

A Training Manual for the Great Commission Usher

Dr. Victor L. Davis

Ushering With A Mission

Orman Press
4200 Sandy Lake Drive, Lithonia, GA 30038

ISBN: 1-891773-44-5

Printed in the United States of America

Dedication

This book is dedicated to my former Minister of Christian Education, Reverend Dr. Florence Canada, whose council aided in the development of this book.

To all the members, especially the Ushers, of the Bethlehem Baptist Church of Richmond, Virginia, and the East End Baptist Church of Sufolk, Virginia, for allowing their services to be an example to others.

To my darling wife, Rosa, who faithfully encouraged me and made this all possible. I love you with all my heart.

Contents

Welcome!

Dear Pastor and Usher Training Leader,

You are holding in your hand the most unique training handbook to be used in the ongoing task of discipling believers. It is the first comprehensive guide that is specifically addressed to the needs of one of the most neglected groups in many of our churches today – the Usher. If you have been in search of a resource that will aid you in addressing the spiritual needs of Ushers, then continue reading.

The traditional approach to ushering focused on the task of "meeting, seating, and greeting" worshippers as they entered the place of worship. The typical training manual addressed the various techniques to be employed as the usher carries out their responsibilities. Although this training manual seeks to address the proper protocol to be employed while the usher carries out his or her duties, *Ushering With A Mission* emphasizes the importance of discipling the individual usher. Ushering is not something we simply do because "it's our Sunday to usher;" rather, it is a lifestyle resulting from the overflow of the "Spirit-filled" life.

The result therefore is a training manual that stresses the importance of Bible study, prayer (both private and corporate), and personal evangelism. Ushers are equipped to share their faith with unbelievers and become active in personal evangelism. They will also find fellowship with other believers in the Body of Christ as they explore ways to fulfill the Great Commission and Commandment of our Lord and Savior, Jesus Christ.

My prayer is that you will find this manual to be a helpful tool in your efforts to equip your Ushers for the "work of the ministry." May God bless the fruit of your labor.

Sincerely,

Victor L. Davis is pastor of the Bethlehem Baptist Church of Richmond, Virginia. Pastor Davis received his Bachelor of Science degree from Norfolk State University in Norfolk, Virginia, Masters of Divinity from Southwestern Baptist Theological Seminary, in Fort Worth, Texas and his Doctor of Ministry degree from Union Theological Seminary in Richmond, Virginia. Dr. Davis's pastoral experience extends over the past 25 years.

In addition to his pastoral responsibilities, Dr. Davis has served as the Director of Black Church Relations for the International Mission Board of the Southern Baptist Convention, formally known as the Foreign Mission Board. Dr. Davis and his wife Rosa are the proud parents of two children, Victor, Jr. and Kristin.

Foreword

Who would ever have imagined the outcome of the discussions of that small group of dedicated members of First Baptist Church. They met to discuss ways to seat worshippers in a more orderly manner. Little did they realize their efforts would turn out to be the embryo of a ministry that now exists in some form in churches around the world – the Usher's Ministry.

As pastor of the historic First Baptist Church South Richmond, located in Richmond, Virginia, I was proud to learn that the first documented evidence of the organization of ushers as a ministry group took place here at First Church in the year 1822. The Ministry of the Usher now stands as one of the most unique contributions of the African-American Church and continues to avail itself as a vessel for those who heed the call of the Master to servant ministry.

Dr. Davis's work in developing this training manual has opened the door for a new and positive approach to the Usher's Ministry. At last, a comprehensive plan for the local church that leads ushers along the path of Christian discipleship. It is a breath of fresh air for those who long to lead their ushers beyond bea a "board" to being a "ministry."

This training tool can help every church, regardless of size or ethnic make-up, become vitally involved in equipping ushers to do their part in fulfilling the Great Commission of our Lord.

Dwight C. Jones
Pastor of the First Baptist Church South Richmond
Richmond, Virginia

An Introduction

There is a story of a man who had recently moved into the Richmond area and found himself shopping at a well known grocery store. The store was very clean and inviting in its appearance. However, more important than the inviting physical appearance of the building was the friendliness of the staff. When he entered the store, someone greeted him with a smile and a warm, "Good Morning. Welcome to Ukrop's." As he was shopping, one of the stock clerks noticed that he was having difficulty trying to find an item on his shopping list and proceeded to help him locate it. When it was time for the man to check out his grocery purchases, one of the employees not only bagged his groceries but took them to his car and loaded them for him. When he attempted to tip the young man for his courteous act, the young man refused the offer and explained that as an employee of the grocery store he was committed to providing the highest quality service to their customers. Therefore, he could not accept a tip for doing what he had pledged to do as a normal part of his job.

The next day the man visited a church. He found it somewhat inconvenient that he had to park a considerable distance away from the building because the parking lot was full of the members' cars. He then noticed that the building was in need of repair. As he walked in, no one greeted him or offered him any assistance in finding his way around the building. Later in the service, he was asked to move out of the seat he was sitting in because it belonged to someone who had been sitting there for years. After the service was over, no one said anything to him as he was leaving or extended an invitation for him to return. He was left with a very cold impression of that church. The man later stated that if he had chosen which of the two institutions to join based on the hospitality he had received, he would have joined the grocery store.

Certainly, we realize that this story may be an extreme example of the importance of hospitality, yet it does serve to illustrate the impact a warm reception and a friendly environment have in creating an inviting atmosphere to a "would be member." The advice to put one's best foot forward ought to be as applicable to churches as it is to individuals, particularly in as much as the church has so much to offer so many people. Ushers are in the strategic position where worshippers obtain first impressions. Therefore, their role is highly significant.

The presence of men and women usher boards, often serving together, serves as a marvelous example of the concept of Christian servanthood at its best.

Unlike in other cultural settings, the usher's ministry in the African-American church setting has gained a unique prominence. Its membership is only exceeded, in many churches, by the music ministry. In many white churches, the presence of women ushers is conspicuously absent. This is not so in the Black church context. The presence of men and women usher boards, often serving together, serves as a marvelous example of the concept of Christian servanthood at its best. It is for the purpose of strengthening and improving the skills of those who serve as ushers in the context of this tradition that this manual is provided. However, we will not limit ourselves to the exploration of the "proper technique" of ushering as many other usher manuals do.

Ushering With A Mission seeks to emphasize the "ministry" aspects of ushering and to offer church leaders a practical guide which expands the role of ushers beyond being "doorkeepers" to being ministers of Him who said, "I am the door..." (John 10:9).

Ushering With A Mission seeks to offer a programmatic way to breathe new life into the body of ushers by challenging them to become "Great Commission Ushers" whose task is to do their part in supporting the mission of the church by discovering ways ushers can become more involved in evangelism, discipleship, ministry, fellowship, worship and stewardship.

It is our prayer that those who use this manual will find it to be a helpful tool that will enhance their effectiveness as they seek joyfully to be "a doorkeeper in this house of the Lord" (Psalm 84:10).

NOTES

CHAPTER ONE

A Biblical Foundation for the Ushers' Ministry

Ushering in the Old Testament

Ushers in the Old Testament tabernacle, and later in the temple, were called "doorkeepers." The Psalmist, who wrote to the chief musician in the temple, understood the importance of ushers when he said, "How amiable are thy tabernacles, O LORD of Hosts!… Blessed are they that dwell in thy house: they will be still praising thee... I had rather be a doorkeeper in the house of my God, than to dwell in the tents of wickedness" (Psalm 84:1,4,10). One of the functions of doorkeepers in the Old Testament was to receive the collections from the people: "Go up to Kilkiah the high priest, that he may sum the silver which is brought into the house of the Lord, which the keepers of the door have gathered of the people" (2 Kings 22:4). Jeremiah refers to one of these doorkeepers as a "man of God." He said, "And I brought them into the house of the Lord, into the chamber of the sons of Hanan, the son of Igdaliah, a man of God, which was by the chamber of the princes, which was above the chamber of Maaseiah the son of Shallum, the keeper of the door" (Jeremiah 35:4). The Old Testament Chronicler wrote of Shallum and his brethren who "were over the work of the service, keepers of the gate of the tabernacle… keepers of the entry" (1 Chronicles 9:19).

The Psalmist, who wrote to the chief musician in the temple, understood the importance of ushers when he said, "How amiable are thy tabernacles, O Lord of Hosts!... Blessed are they that dwell in thy house: they will be still praising thee.... I had rather be a doorkeeper in the house of my God, than to dwell in the tents of wickedness" (Psalm 84:1,4,10).

The preacher in Ecclesiastes wrote about "the day when the keepers of the house shall tremble" (Ecclesiastes 12:3). And in Ezekiel's version of a future temple, he saw space reserved for the priests, the musicians, and two sets of ushers: "The keepers of the charge of the house," and "the keepers of the charge of the altar" (Ezekiel 40:44, 46).

Ushering in the New Testament

In the New Testament, the temple ushers were given unusual authority, evidently as uniformed guards. In the Acts of the Apostles, "the captain of the temple" and "the officers" are referred to several times in connection with arrests and general handling of the crowds. It was these doorkeepers or ushers, who carried out the orders of the high priests in the persecutions in the temple against the Apostles immediately following Pentecost and 30 years later in the arrests and maltreatment of Saint Paul.

Jesus had His disciples function as ushers on many occasions. They prepared the way for His coming.

Jesus had His disciples function as ushers on many occasions. They prepared the way for His coming. They introduced people to Him and in general directed the people who had come to hear Him speak or to be touched by His healing hands. On one occasion, Jesus gave a sharp warning to the disciples, who, as ushers, had endeavored to keep children away from the Master (Matthew 19:13-15). On still another occasion, Jesus directed the disciples in organizing a congregation of 5,000 men plus women and children, to be seated in groups of 50. Then, with Christ supplying the unending loaves and fishes, the disciples served the hungry multitude (Mark 6:33-44).

Acts 6 records the response of the apostle to a dilemma that was hindering their effectiveness in ministry. "Then the twelve called the multitude of disciples unto them and said, it is not reason that we should leave the Word of God and serve tables. Wherefore, brethren, look ye out among you seven men...whom we may appoint over this business. But we will give ourselves continually to prayer, and to the ministry of the word. And the saying pleased the multitude" (Acts 6:2-5). The traditional approach to the interpretation of this passage has viewed it as being the beginning of the deacons ministry. However, the ministry of the seven could also serve as a role model for the ushers ministry in that they allowed the Holy Spirit to guide them in their ministry to the needs of the congregation.

Biblical Characteristics of a Good Usher

The three qualities of good men explained by Jesus in the Sermon on the Mount could not be more applicable to the ministry of church ushers. First, the ministry of ushering is like salt which makes everything more palatable and which serves as a general preservative against deterioration. Jesus did not say, "Ye ought to be the salt of the earth," but He said "Ye are the salt of the earth" (Matthew 5:13). Consequently, ushers enjoy the ministry of constructive influence. Paul said, "Let your speech be always with grace, seasoned with salt" (Colossians 4:6). A good usher adds a tang of joy to a churchgoer's Sunday morning experience instead of a tinge of dread. Also, the ministry of an usher is like salt because salt can never do its work until it is brought into close contact with the substance on which it is to make its influence. The church ushers come into direct contact on an individual basis with more people in a given service than anyone else who ministers to them. The ministry of salt is silent, inconspicuous, and sometimes completely unnoticed. But it is there, in a powerful and useful way.

Ushers enjoy the ministry of constructive influence.

Like salt, a good usher also is like "a city set upon a hill" (Matthew 5:14). While ushers are like inconspicuous salt, they also may become like a city on a hill. They become landmarks to churchgoers who learn to depend upon them. Stability helps overcome many other weaknesses in the priority of qualifications among ushers. The first glimpse of an usher on whom a churchgoer has come to depend brings an internal sense of welcome response; they feel that someone is on hand who is interested in me! It is not uncommon for an usher to become an advisor, a source of information, counselor, or better yet, an intermediary between the needs of a specific person and the resources available through pastor, musicians and teachers of the church.

Third, a good usher is like a lamp on a stand, not put "under a bushel but on a candlestick; and it giveth light unto all that are in the house" (Matthew 5:15). A lamp brings warmth and welcome to all who are in the room. One flickering candle can brighten the conversation in a room and bring an inner feeling of warmth and joy. As a lamp dispels the darkness and brings emotional warmth to a room, so the ministry of an usher can make a similar intangible contribution to all who experience the inner light of pleasure in people which the usher allows to shine through him/herself. Jesus concluded this discussion in the character of a good usher by saying, "Let your light so shine before men, that they may see your good works, and glorify your Father which is in Heaven" (Matthew 5:16). It is the nature of Christian character to radiate; it cannot help but shine. But the radiance of this glory is not for "self" but for the kingdom of God. The ministry of an usher is not intended to bring glory to self but to God. Just as a pastor preaches in the Spirit, and a musician sings in the Spirit, the usher must usher in the power of the Holy Spirit, bringing glory to God in the Lord's house on the Lord's day.

A Biblical Foundation for the Usher's Ministry

1. David wrote in Psalm 84:10, "I would rather be a ________________________ in the house of my God, than to dwell in the tents of ________________________.

2. In the New Testament, the temple ushers were given authority as uniformed ________________________.

3. Jesus had his ________________________ function as ushers, as they prepared the way for His coming.

4. In Acts 6, the ministry of the seven can serve as a model for ________________________ as well as for ________________________.

5. The three biblical characteristics of a good usher are:

   A. They must be "the ________________________ of the earth" (Matthew 5:13).

   B. A good usher is like "a ____________________ set upon a hill" (Matthew 5:14).

   C. A good usher is like a ________________________ on a stand, not put "under a bushel but on a ________________________..." (Matthew 5:15).

6. The ministry of the usher is to bring glory to ________________________.

NOTES

CHAPTER TWO

The Modern Day Ushers' Movement

At the time research was being done on the development of this manual, the earliest documented evidence of the existence of an ushers' ministry could be traced to the First Baptist Church South Richmond. Records indicate the existence of ushers in that church since 1822. Typical of the culture of that day, the ushers were men only. It was not uncommon for ushers to be deacons since they served to collect the offering. It wasn't until 1928 that a little noticed, yet significant, event took place with the appointment of women to serve as ushers. This addition of the Ladies Auxiliary would stand as one of the unique distinctions of the African-American church and the role women would play in its growth and development.

> ***...the philosophy of ushering as, "... the art of making the church member and visitor feel comfortable at home and of lending spiritual dignity to the whole church service."***

A search of the history of ushering during modern times could not be complete without reference to the contributions of the great Evangelist, Dwight L. Moody. This shoe salesman turned Evangelist (1837-99) found the large audiences that came to hear the gospel no small challenge. Moody, who daily crammed 11,000 people into his New York meetings over a four-month period in early 1876, saw ushering as an answer to crowd-control management. Moody was particular about his ushers and personally hired 500 men to seat the crowds at the New York revival.

Ambrose Clark has the distinction of formally establishing the first church ushers association. Clark crystallized the philosophy of ushering as, "... the art of making the church member and visitor feel comfortable at home and of lending spiritual dignity to the whole church service." The Church Ushers' Association of New York was formally established on January 19, 1914.

Currently, ushers' unions exist in 25 states with a national membership that exceeds 150,000 members.

The Modern Day Usher's Movement

1. The earliest evidence of an usher's ministry was traced to the First Baptist Church South Richmond, Virginia in the year ________________________.

2. At that time there were only ________________________ ushers.

3. One of the unique distinctions of the African-American church was the appointment of ________________________ to serve as ushers in the year ________.

4. In 1876, Evangelist Dwight L. Moody, saw ushering as an answer to ________________________ control due to his large audiences.

5. ________________________ has distinction of formally establishing the first Church Ushers' Association in ________________________.

6. His philosophy of ushering was "...making the church member and visitor feel ________________________ at home and of lending ________________________ dignity to the whole church service."

NOTES

CHAPTER THREE

The Great Commission Usher

If there is a single verse that characterizes the purpose of the church it must be Matthew 28:18-20:

"And Jesus came and spoke unto them, saying, All power is given unto me in heaven and in earth. Go ye therefore, and teach all nations, baptizing them in the name of the Father, and of the Son, and of the Holy Ghost: Teaching them to observe all things whatsoever I have commanded you: and, lo, I am with you always, even unto the end of the world. Amen."

We have come to know this verse as the Great Commission. These words spoken by our Savior serve as the marching orders for the church. When we take into consideration the teachings of scripture in its entirety, we can identify functions. These functions are worship, discipleship, evangelism, fellowship and ministry. All that we do as a church should relate to one of these functions. Every time we gather, every time we open the doors of the church building, every ounce of our expended energy as followers of Christ ought to, in some way, be the outgrowth of one or more of these tasks. Even as we usher, we should do so with an evangelistic, disciplined, ministering, fellowshipping, worshipping and stewarding motivation. Our ushering should be done with a mission, and that is the fulfillment of the Great Commission.

...as we usher, we should do so with an evangelistic, disciplined, ministering, fellowshipping, worshipping and stewarding motivation. Our ushering should be done with a mission, and that is the fulfillment of the Great Commission.

It is at this point that we see the distinctiveness of the *Ushering With A Mission* model for the ushers' ministry. Unlike other usher manuals that limit their discussion to the mechanics of ushering, *Ushering With A Mission* not only provides adequate instruction on proper ushering techniques, but it also offers a practical guide for church leaders that equip ushers with skills in sharing their faith. The ushers' meeting becomes not only the setting for conducting the business of the usher board, but it also serves as an opportunity for disciplining new Christians in the faith. Ushers will be challenged to discover how they can use their spiritual gifts and talents to start or strengthen new and/or existing ministries. *Ushering With A Mission* will lead participants in discovering new ways to minister to the needs of youth through the youth usher board. *Ushering With A Mission* truly represents the first programmatic approach toward strengthening the ministry of ushering.

The remaining chapters in this manual will provide you with an understanding of how to move beyond the traditional usher board to being "Great Commission Ushers" ushering with a mission for Christ.

The Great Commission Usher

1. The purpose of the church was spoken by our Savior in Matthew 28:18-20, is known as the __________________ __________________ __________________.

2. The five marching orders of the church are:

A. ____

B. ____

C. ____

D. ____

E. ____

3. *Ushering With A Mission* challenges ushers to discover how they can use their spiritual ____________________ and ____________________ to start or strengthen new and/or existing ministries.

4. This training manual will provide you with an understanding of how to move beyond the traditional usher board to being

"__________________ __________________ __________________,"

__________________ __________________ __________________

__________________ for Christ.

NOTES

CHAPTER FOUR

The Usher and Worship

Worship is awesome and breathtaking! It is an encounter with the living God as we enter into His holy and magnificent presence. Worship is also a time of celebration as we take time to reflect upon all that God has done in our lives individually and corporately. As we worship, we express our adoration and reverence for God.

The worship of God is the foundation upon which is built all that the Christian usher is and does. Our worship of God is, in essence, an intimate relationship with God out of which everything flows. It has a private dimension as well as a communal dimension. The private dimension is exercised as each one of us communes with God in our "secret closet" during times of private devotion. The communal dimension is exercised when we come together as a body of believers for times of corporate worship. Both forms of worship are essential for a balanced spiritual life.

> ***The worship of God is the foundation upon which is built all that the Christian usher is and does.***

Private or communal, the actual manifestation of worship may take many different forms. This speaks to the uniqueness which God has created within every human being. Shouting, singing, weeping, dancing, prayer, preaching, the reading of the Word and sitting quietly are all valid forms of worship. Indeed, Psalm 100 encourages us to "make a joyful noise, worship with gladness, sing, be thankful, praise God and bless Him." It has a private dimension as well as a communal dimension. The private dimension is exercised as each one of us communes with God in our "secret closet" during times of private devotion. The communal dimension is exercised when we come together as a body of believers for times of corporate worship. Both forms of worship are essential for a balanced spiritual life.

Psalm 100:5 reads, "The Lord is good; his steadfast love endures forever, and his faithfulness to all generations." God is good and worship provides believers the opportunity to acknowledge and respond to His goodness. We respond by offering ourselves back to Him for His service. Thus, worship provides an opportunity to recommit and rededicate ourselves to God.

It is through worship that we are energized, revitalized and empowered to go forth serving, sharing, and loving in the name of Jesus Christ. It is through worship that our spiritual tanks are refilled. It is through worship that our relationship with God is strengthened (Isaiah 40:31). It is through worship, as we commune with God, that we receive guidance and direction which enables us to serve Him faithfully and obediently. Thus, worship is a transforming experience. And as we are transformed, we confess our sins to a loving and forgiving God. Worship challenges us to change our hearts, minds and lives. Our transformation is essential and is how God molds and shapes us for His service.

It is through worship, as we commune with God, that we receive guidance and direction which enables us to serve Him faithfully and obediently.

Worship is essential for all persons who are committed to living a life committed and dedicated to serving God. Worship is essential for those who are serious about growing in their knowledge and understanding of who God is. Worship is essential for those seeking a deeper and more personal relationship with God. Without worship, it is impossible to be faithful in our service of God. This is why a strong and consistent devotional life focused around prayer and Bible study is important to the usher. These times will help the usher grow in knowledge and understanding of God and God's will for his/her life. This includes God's will as it pertains to the ministry of ushering. These times will strengthen the usher to go forth serving in a godly manner. These times will fortify the usher and help prepare him/her to minister with love even in difficult and trying situations.

As a part of a strong devotional life, the usher is encouraged to be in prayer for other ushers, church members and church concerns. Prayer should also be a part of the usher's ritual as he/she prepares to take the assigned post and even while ushering. Many usher boards have an usher's prayer which all members learn. This prayer may be used as part of their preparation or during ushers' meetings. Indeed, the usher's entire demeanor and attitude needs to be one of prayer.

The usher is in charge of the flow of traffic during the worship service. Thus, it is important to know how to seat persons. In general, it is good practice to seat persons as near to the front and center of the sanctuary as possible. This way, the back pews are reserved for late-comers. By properly seating persons as they enter for worship, persons are able to take their seats without having to climb over other worshippers and with as little disturbance as possible to the flow of worship. It can also be a good practice to whisper to the worshipper where you plan to seat him/her before beginning up the aisle. Avoid asking people where they would like to sit. The usher should always be alert, attentive and aware of persons needing to be seated. The usher should never point seats out or allow a person to wander off down the aisle alone. It is also important to know when and when not to let persons enter and exit the sanctuary. Most churches have pauses or interludes built into their worship services to allow for the entrance of late-comers. Late-comers should be allowed to enter during these pauses and seated as quickly and inconspicuously as possible. In general, persons should limit movement during scripture reading, prayer, singing and offertory. It is advised that ushers check with the pastor or other worship leader for preferred times of movement. When persons desire to enter and exit during these times, the usher should tactfully and politely ask them to wait. As the facilitator of traffic during the worship service, it is important for the usher to know that the pulpit area is holy and sacred ground. Thus, it is important to show the proper respect for this area. It is the ushers responsibility not to let anyone cross in front of the pulpit once worship has started, especially when someone is speaking or the minister is preaching.

During corporate worship, the usher is a worshipper as well as a facilitator for worship which is reverent and holy. Indeed, even as the usher greets members and allows them to enter the sanctuary, it is important to realize that those who enter are being ushered into the very presence of God. Thus, the usher plays a pivotal role in our efforts to make sure our worship is God-focused and God-centered.

Serving as opportunities for spiritual renewal, ushers in almost every church have an annual anniversary. This is a time when ushers may be ministered to and participate more freely in worship. Anniversary services provide a unique opportunity for ushers to worship God in "spirit and in truth" (John 4:23-24). During these services, guest ushers usually come in so the ushers who are celebrating can "take the day off." Indeed, ushers are encouraged to make sure the "anniversary" is a time for focusing on God and celebrating His goodness, glorifying Him and lifting Him up.

The Usher and Worship

1. The foundation upon which all that the Christian usher is and does is the ____________ of ____________.

2. Worship is an encounter with the living God as we enter and experience His ____________ and ____________.

3. As we worship, we express our ____________ and ____________ for God.

4. Worship takes many forms such as: ____________, ____________, ____________, ____________, ____________, ____________, ____________, and ____________.

5. In ____________, we are encouraged to make a joyful noise unto the Lord.

6. Worship provides an opportunity to ____________ and ____________ to God's goodness.

7. Worship also gives us an opportunity to ____________ our sins.

8. A strong and consistent devotional life focused around ____________ and ____________ will help the usher grow in their knowledge of God and His will for his/her life.

9. It is important for ushers to remember that when they allow members to enter the sanctuary, the members are being ushered into the very ____________ of God.

10. During the worship service, the usher is in charge of the flow of ____________.

11. The usher should always be ________________, ________________ and ________________ of persons needing to be seated.

12. Persons should not be allowed to enter or exit during:

    A. ____

    B. ____

    C. ____

    D. ____

13. The _________________________ area is holy and sacred ground during the worship service.

14. The "Usher's Anniversary" should be a time for focusing on God and celebrating His _________________________.

15. As a facilitator of worship, the usher's role is to make sure worship is _________________________ and _________________________.

NOTES

CHAPTER FIVE

The Usher and Discipleship

Discipleship, follow-up, and conversation, these are all terms for what Gary W. Kuhne calls "the spiritual work of grounding a new believer in the faith." Such training involves developing continuous spiritual maturity (both inwardly in relationship to God and outwardly in relationships with other people) and spiritual reproductiveness in a Christian's life.

Kuhne, in his book, *The Dynamics of Personal Follow-Up*, defines a disciple as "a Christian who is growing in conformity to Christ, is achieving fruit in evangelism, and is working in follow-up to conserve his fruit." Personal follow-up can occur when a mature Christian assumes a one-on-one relationship with a new Christian to aid the new Christian in his/her nurture and growth toward Christ-likeness.

The primary goal of the Christian life is to become like Jesus – to have a Christ-like character. "Till we all come in the unity of the faith, and of the knowledge of the Son of God unto a perfect man, unto the measure of the stature of the fullness of Christ: That we henceforth be no more children...but speaking the truth in love, may grow up into Him in all things, which is the head, even Christ (Ephesians 4:13-15). A person of this maturity is one who is walking daily in the Spirit and, thereby, manifesting the fruit of the Spirit. The Holy Spirit produces within us a complete (Colossians 2:9-10), consistent (Galatians 5:22-25), and Christ-like (Galatians 4:19) character which is outwardly expressed by the bearing of fruit.

It is imperative from the beginning to understand that discipleship training is not a method – it is the transferring of a lifestyle. It is, in essence, the Master's method to bring the world to himself – to usher in His kingdom. In the *Master Plan of Evangelism* by Robert Coleman, the explanation of Jesus' strategy clarifies much about our responsibilities as his disciples. His first method was the selection of a few, who were willing learners, out of the masses. He did not neglect the masses. He continued to minister to them, but he chose a few to concentrate upon – to train intensively. Once this was accomplished,

Christ spent time in close association with them. He called the twelve "that they might be with Him" (Mark 3:14). The disciples "caught" true discipleship more than they were "taught" it. They were with Jesus, watching His responses and actions in every sort of situation. They were walking with a "living example" of God. To be godly, they had only to imitate – understanding came later.

Another of Christ's methods was consecration. He required and expected obedience, not intellect. He required discipline and the cross. Needless to say, it "thinned the crowd," but the result was eleven men who brought news which shook the world. This method is known as spiritual multiplication. A mature Christian trains and nurtures a babe in Christ, then sends him/her out to win and train another. For example, if you took six months to train a young Christian before sending him/her out and then the two of you continued in this work of winning, training and sending, at the end of only three years you would have trained sixty-four disciples who are able to train others. At the end of five years the number would be 1,024.

The Bible teaches that the Christian has both and inward and outward need for discipleship training. A Christian must first desire to become a disciple in an inward journey. He/she must be willing to learn. Jesus said, "Take my yoke upon you and learn of me" (Matthew 12:29). A disciple of Christ seeks to mature in the faith. The writer of Hebrews compares a Christian who never grows up to a baby that never gets past a milk diet in what he is able to digest. "For when for the time ye ought to be teachers ye have need that one teach you again which be the first principles of the oracles of God; and are become such as have need of milk, and not of strong meat" (Hebrews 5:12). The evidence of discipleship is in the lifestyle. "… but as he which hath called you is holy, so be ye holy in all manner of conversation; because it is written, be ye holy for I am holy" (1 Peter 1:15-16). These are the inward manifestations.

A Christian is also called to outward discipleship to witness and teach. We are to be a witness. As Jesus was walking along the shore of the sea of Galilee, He saw Peter and Andrew casting a net into the sea, and He said to them, "Follow me and I will make you fishers of men" (Matthew 4:19). We must live out our faith in such a way that others can see the results of discipleship. The book of James has been called a manual of Christian living. He says, "Be ye doers of the word and not hearers only, deceiving your own selves"

(James 1:22). The last words of Jesus before He ascended to the Father is called The Great Commission. It is our marching orders as disciples. "Go ye therefore, and teach all nations, baptizing them in the name of the Father, and of the Son, and of the Holy Ghost: teaching them to observe all things whatsoever I have commanded you; and lo, I am with you always, even unto the end of the world. Amen." (Matthew 28:19-20). There is no doubt from the general message of the Bible that the Christian is to mature in Christ and reach out to the world.

Perhaps the greatest single principle in making disciples is the "follow me" principle. This is the principle of setting the example: embodying what you desire to teach, setting the pace, leading out in what you want the person you are discipling to do. You do this and ask him/her to follow you. Notice how Paul did this:

I. By Example and Pacesetting – Being and Doing – A godly man pressing on

"... you know what kind of men we proved be among you for your sake." (1 Thessalonians 1:5)

He set the pace. Why? "for your sake." Notice the emphasis on this in 1 Timothy 4:12, Titus 2:7,8, Titus 1:5ff; 1 Timothy 3:1-7; and 1 Thessalonians 2:10-12.

II. Get Them To Follow You

"And you became followers of us, and of the Lord" (1 Thessalonians 1:6).

Do not try to hide behind humility. If you're thinking, "I don't feel good enough to be followed," it is unscriptural. Jesus said, "Follow me" (Mark 1:17-20; 3:14). He ordained twelve to be "with Him." Paul did exactly this. He said, "Be ye followers of me, even as I also am of Christ." (1 Corinthians 11:1). When we follow Christ, we need not fear to tell others to follow us. Notice again and again this emphasis in 1 Corinthians 4:16; Philippians 3:17 and 4:9; 2 Corinthians 12:18; 2 Thessalonians 3: 7,9 and Hebrews 6:12.

Ask them to do what you do in witnessing. Ask them to do what you do in your devotional life. As they follow you, you love them and share your life with them (1 Thessalonians 2:7-14). Paul said, "I kept back nothing that was profitable unto you..." (Acts 20:20).

III. They Become Examples to Others as You are to Them

"So that ye were ensamples to all that believe in Macedonia and Achaia." (1 Thessalonians 1:7)

Share your life with them and God will give you those who will become examples to others. Remember that we are after spiritual multiplication. Notice Paul's fear of "laboring in vain." Galatians 4:11; Philippians 2:16; 2 Corinthians 6:1; 1 Thessalonians 3:5.

As an usher, it is important to be actively and intentionally involved in the inward or personal part of discipleship. Indeed, as a follower of Jesus Christ, every usher has the responsibility to strive daily to be more Christ-like. Indeed, a disciplined lifestyle which includes, prayer, Bible study, and worship will help the usher to meet the task of ushering with a smile and a willing heart. However, it is also important for the ushers' ministry to be systematically and intentionally involved in the outward aspect of discipleship. In other words, it is important for ushers to seek to disciple others. One opportunity to disciple others comes when new members join an usher board. Every new usher should be assigned to a seasoned usher who can help him/her grow and develop in the techniques of ushering as well as spiritual maturity.

As an usher, it is important to be actively and intentionally involved in the inward or personal part of discipleship.

Jesus shared an eye-opening insight with us about discipleship when He says, "The disciple is not above his teacher: but every one when he is perfected shall be as his teacher" (Luke 6:40). It is paramount that before you ever enter into a discipling relationship with another person, you first count the cost of being a disciple. It involves priority, commitment, and time. In this position, you will be serving as a role model, good or bad, for new believers. They will need contact with you in many different situations, any of which, might become their "teachable moment," the point at which their minds begin to "click" regarding the truths you have been teaching. You, like Christ and like Paul, will become their example.

Now do not let that scare you. If all Christians wait until they are perfect, discipleship will never be more than an idealistic fantasy. However, do let it make you aware of your responsibilities. No program, follow-up schedule, Bible study, or memorization plan, no matter how dynamic, will ever have the spiritual impact on a new believer as your genuine "agape" love for him/her and your totally "sold out" example lived before them.

Jesus Christ has offered to each of us His total victory over Satan and this world.

Just remember, in discipleship, you are "growing" a person to be like your Master, Christ. You imitate engendering life habits which exemplify His life. This implies that you know your Master very personally and have a consistent and close walk with Him. You must portray His likeness daily. Mission Impossible? No! Jesus Christ has offered to each of us His total victory over Satan and this world. We need only claim it, breathe it, walk in it, and live it by faith. Are you ready to try? Good!

The Usher and Discipleship

1. "The spiritual work of grounding a new believer in the faith" is called ______________________.

2. The primary goal of the Christian life is to become like ______________________.

3. Discipleship training is not a method, it is the transferring of a ______________________.

4. Jesus' first method of discipleship focused on the ______________________ of a few who were willing learners.

5. He then spent time in close ______________________ with them.

6. Another method of Christ was ______________________, it is known as spiritual multiplication.

7. A mature Christian ______________________ and ______________________ a babe in Christ.

8. A disciple of Christ seeks to ______________________ in the faith.

9. Jesus told Peter and Andrew, "______________________ me" and he would make them "______________________" of men.

10. We must live out our faith in such a way that others can see the results of ______________________.

11. Jesus' words, "Go ye therefore, and teach all nations, baptizing them in the name of the Father..." is called the ______________________ ______________________.

12. The greatest single principle in making disciples is the "______________________" principle.

13. The disciplined lifestyle includes ________________________,
________________________, and ________________________.

14. As a new usher joins the ministry, he should be assigned a seasoned usher who encourages him/her to ________________________ and ________________________ in the techniques of ushering.

15. The cost of being a disciple involves ________________________,
________________________, and ________________________.

16. In discipleship you are "________________________" a person to be like your
________________________.

NOTES

CHAPTER SIX

The Usher and Evangelism

Evangelism is the act of sharing which takes place when believers share the "good news" of Jesus Christ with those who have not yet accepted Christ as Lord and Savior of their life. This act of sharing is sometimes referred to as witnessing or sharing our faith.

> ***Evangelism is really a matter of life and death.***

What is good news? Jesus lives! Jesus heals! Jesus saves! Jesus empowers! Jesus frees! Jesus loves! Jesus shows us the way! Jesus cares! The good news is the difference a relationship with Jesus Christ can make in a person's life. Central to the good news is what Jesus did for us on the cross. For it is through His sacrificial death on the cross that we are saved. It is through the power of His shed blood that we are cleansed and redeemed. It is because of Jesus' death on the cross and subsequent resurrection that we can be sure of ultimate victory over death and the gift of eternal life. Thus, we can exclaim with the apostle Paul, "Where, O death is your victory? Where, O death is your sting?" (1 Corinthians 15:56).

Evangelism is really a matter of life and death. For there are many men, women, boys and girls who do not know Jesus Christ. There are many who have never heard the good news. There are many who are held captive to sin because they do not know Jesus has already purchased their freedom through His shed blood on the cross. Indeed, how can they know unless someone shares the good news with them?

We were not saved solely that we might live life and live it more abundantly. We were saved to share the good news with others. It is through Jesus Christ that we are reconciled unto God. As His disciples, it is our responsibility to join Jesus in the work of reconciliation (2 Corinthians 5: 17-20):

> *Therefore if any man be in Christ, he is a new creature: old things are passed away; behold, all things are become new.*
>
> *And all things are of God, who hath reconciled us to himself by*

Jesus Christ, and hath given to us the ministry of reconciliation;

To wit, that God was in Christ, reconciling the world unto himself, not imputing their trespasses unto them; and hath committed unto us the word of reconciliation.

Now then we are ambassadors for Christ, as though God did beseech you by us: we pray you in Christ's stead, be ye reconciled to God.

Indeed, it is through evangelism that we help God's kingdom grow. As we share the good news of Jesus Christ – as we lead others to salvation, God's kingdom grows.

Every person who has accepted Jesus Christ as Lord and Savior has a responsibility to be actively involved in evangelism. It is impossible to follow Jesus Christ and not share the good news. Indeed, Jesus, in Matthew 28:19-20, commanded all of his disciples to go forth sharing the good news. Failing to be actively involved in evangelism is to fail to obey Jesus. Failing to be actively involved in evangelism is to condemn countless others to eternal death. Failing to be actively involved in evangelism is to deny what Jesus has done in our life. It is to deny our relationship with Him.

Evangelism is the means by which we witness. Our witness, or the sharing of our faith, goes beyond mere words. Our witness is our life and our life is our witness. Indeed, our witness comes out of our personal experience. It shows, tells or gives evidence of the things we have experienced. Thus, our witness of Jesus Christ should give evidence of personal experiences with Him.

The usher is in a position to evangelize.

Daily, we find ourselves in situations which provide opportunities to give witness to what Jesus Christ has done in our lives. This is also true for the usher. Every time an usher assumes his/her post, that usher is in a position to witness for Jesus Christ. The usher is in a position to evangelize.

Let me make it simple. If you have experienced the love of Jesus in your life, demonstrate that love to others with a kind word, a warm smile, or a nod of encouragement. If you are free in Christ Jesus, walk with upright posture, head held high and confident steps. If you love the Lord, serve Him and your brothers and sisters with joy. When you encounter the occasional person who doesn't want to cooperate (insists on sitting in a particular place or gets upset because he/she has to wait for an appropriate time to enter or exit the sanctuary, for example), do not get upset or engage in self pity. Look to the cross and remember that Jesus lived, died and rose for all without partiality or respect of person. Take pride in what you are doing. If you are a new creature in Christ Jesus, carry out your duties and responsibilities in a manner which glorifies God. Remember, the usher does not just represent self or even the church where they serve. The usher represents God.

> ***The usher represents God.***

Many times, the usher is the first person a visitor encounters. The manner in which the visitor is greeted can have a life-altering impact, especially if the visitor is not saved. To the visitor, the usher represents the church. The usher represents all Christians. The usher represents Jesus. If the ushers' witness exhibits the Christ in them, the visitor will be drawn. If Christ is not exhibited, the visitor will be turned off.

Ushers, be ever mindful of the witness you are giving for you never know who you are greeting at the door. Your greeting and your service can be the determining factor which leads a person to accept Jesus Christ as Lord and Savior. It can also be the determining factor in a lost person's decision to remain lost.

In closing, ushers be sure your witness is an accurate representation of all you have experienced in Christ Jesus and God will be glorified. God's kingdom will grow, your church will grow and you will be blessed.

The Usher and Evangelism

1. Evangelism is the act of sharing which takes place when believers share the "_______________ _______________" of Jesus Christ.

2. This act of evangelism is sometimes referred to as _______________ or _______________ our faith.

3. The good news is the difference a _______________ with Jesus Christ can make in one's life.

4. The good news is that through the power of His shed blood we are _______________ and _______________.

5. We were saved to live life _______________, and to _______________ the good news with others.

6. It is through _______________that we help God's kingdom grow.

7. In our witness of Jesus Christ, we should give evidence of a personal _______________ with Him.

8. The usher does not represent self or the church, the usher represents _______________.

9. The manner in which a visitor is greeted in the church can have a _______________-altering impact, if the visitor is not saved.

10. If the usher's witness exhibit's the _______________ in him/her, then the visitor will be drawn.

NOTES

CHAPTER SEVEN

The Usher and Fellowship

There is a television sitcom named "Cheers" that at one time was a top-rated comedy. The basic storyline of the show featured the comedic antics of a cast of characters who either worked or frequented a bar named, "Cheers." I did not spend too much time watching the show or following the storyline, yet I found myself intrigued by the words of the theme song played at the beginning of the show. In essence, the songster expresses his desire to find a place filled with people who can offer him a listening ear and a word of support at the end of a hard day, a place where he is known and cared for, a place "where everyone knows my name."

Let me make it clear that I am not endorsing the show nor the method the writer suggests for finding relief from all one's worries. However, I do suggest that the writer of the theme song has expressed the deep longing of many to find his or her place among a community of caring, understanding, supporting persons who share the common need to be loved and accepted. I have often felt that the theme song from "Cheers" in some small way describes what the community of Christ called the church ought to be, a place where everyone knows your name. It is the place where we should be able to find the community of caring, understanding and supporting individuals who have all experienced the same saving grace and mercy of God through Jesus, and have been brought into a unique relationship as family by virtue of that common bond in Christ Jesus. The Biblical term that describes this unique relationship is "fellowship."

As the body of Christ, the church in its essential and primary nature, is a spiritual fellowship (*koinonia*), or familyhood. Jesus gathered a group of believers about himself during his ministry. This group was the church in its incipient stage. To this group was added at Pentecost about three thousand souls. "And they continued steadfastly in the apostles' teaching and fellowship, in the breaking of bread and the prayers. And fear came upon every soul; and many wonders and signs are done through the apostles. And all that believed were together, and had all things common" (Acts 2:42-44). They shared their possessions so that none had need of anything. Day after day they continued to meet and worship together in the temple with one accord praising God, and having favor with all the people (Acts 2:46-47). This exemplifies the true nature of the church. Paul exhibited this same spirit of concern for the poor saints in Jerusalem by receiving a collection of money for them from the churches in Galatia and Greece (1 Corinthians 16:1). This spirit of fellowship, or brotherhood, that characterized the early New Testament church has been true of all Christians of succeeding ages to the degree that they are truly Christians.

The basis of Christian fellowship is Christ Himself. The members of the church have fellowship with one another, because they have experienced a spiritual union with the risen Savior. They are a sanctuary of God where the Spirit of God dwells. To destroy this sanctuary is to be destroyed by God (1 Corinthians 3:17). The Lord's Supper was a participation in the body and the blood of Christ (1 Corinthians 10:16), and was to be observed in a worthy manner (1 Corinthians 11:27-30). Members had been baptized into the one body (1 Corinthians 12:13), and were not to seek their own, but each their neighbor's good (1 Corinthians 10:24). Factions and divisions in the church destroy the fellowship, divide the body of Christ, and bring sickness and even death to those who cause them. Christians were to give no occasion of stumbling to either Jews or Greeks, or the church of God (1 Corinthians 10:32).

In Ephesians and Colossians, Paul presents the church in its spiritual relation to Christ. It is Christ's body in sacred and vital connection with Him, its founder and head. This glorious church as presented in Ephesians, is united, one family, where all barriers of race, culture and social status are broken down. Christ had broken down the barriers between Jew and Gentile, and in Him the two had become one new man reconciled in the fellowship of one body unto God through the cross. This family of believers, united in Christ, constituted the household of God, a holy temple in the Lord for a habitation of God in the Spirit (Ephesians 2). The body shares the heavenly life of the exalted head even now (Ephesians 1:22; 5:27). Yet, this body of Christ lives in the world of sordid reality and must fight to maintain the Christian attitude and action consonant with its position and calling. Paul makes this clear in the worthy walk of Christians portrayed in Ephesians 4-6.

The church is a spiritual fellowship composed of saved people. To the church at Jerusalem, the Lord added day by day those that were being saved (Acts 2:47). Paul calls these saved people "the saints" (Romans 2:7; 1 Corinthians 1:2; 2 Corinthians 1:1; Ephesians 1:1; Colossians 1:1; Philippians. 1:1). The word "saint" is the translation of the Greek adjective "hagios" which means a "holy one", or "human beings consecrated to God." The Greek verb "hagiadzo" means to "consecrate, dedicate, sanctify," and "to purify." A saint, then, is one who has been sanctified, or made holy. Every Christian is a saint, separated to God.

Saints are persons who have been saved by grace through faith in Jesus (Ephesians 2:8). They have been regenerated, or born anew (John 2:3-5), and are children of God being born "not of blood, nor of the will of the flesh, nor of the will of man, but of God" (John 1:13).

Christians are saved people in union with Christ. Jesus had this in mind when he said, "I am the living bread which came down out of heaven: If any man eat of this bread, he shall live forever" (John 6:51). "He that eateth my flesh and drinketh my blood abideth in me, and I in him" (John 6:56). Paul refers to this union when he speaks of being "in Christ," and Christ being in the believer. "So we, who are many, are one body in Christ" (Romans 12:5). "There is therefore now no condemnation to them that are in Christ Jesus" (Romans 8:1). "And if Christ is in you, the body is dead because of sin" (Romans 8:10). "I have been crucified with Christ; and it is no longer I that live, but Christ liveth in me" (Galatians 2:20). This is a spiritual union which lasts forever.

These saved people, in union with Christ, have had their sins forgiven by God (Acts 2:39, 10:43; Ephesians 1:7), have been justified by God on the basis of the atoning work of Christ (Romans 3:23-26; 6:7; 8:33), reconciled to God (Romans 5:10-11), and adopted into the family of God as sons (Romans 8:14, 15; Ephesians 1:5; Galatians 4:4-5).

The church as the body of Christ, is a spiritual fellowship or community of redeemed people who have identified themselves by baptism with His death, burial and resurrection. This sense of community should be evident in every ministry in the church. Thus, those who are a part of the ushers' ministry must strive to develop a sense of community and fellowship where genuine love, care, concern and nurture is provided for every member.

It is very important to have an intentional system for contacting members who miss meetings. It is also important to assist those who experience sickness, death, or other hardships. Indeed, many times ushers can serve as eyes and ears for the pastor to let him/her know situations or circumstances which may require his attention.

Ushers must also be careful not to allow themselves to crystallize into social groups or become isolated from the mainstream of church fellowship. When this happens, it can become difficult to reach out to new members who become a part of the ushers' ministry. This can also cause ushers to lose focus in terms of their overall purpose and mission as a part of the church and as followers of Jesus Christ.

The Usher and Fellowship

1. A community of caring, understanding, supporting individuals who have all experienced the saving grace and mercy of Jesus Christ is called ________________________.

2. The basis of Christian fellowship is ________________________ Himself.

3. Factions and divisions in the church can ________________________ the fellowship, divide the body of Christ, and bring ________________________ and ________________________ to those who cause them.

4. The church in Ephesians existed with all barriers of ________________________, ________________________ and ________________________ are broken down.

5. The word "saint" translated in Greek means "________________________" or "________________________ consecrated to God."

6. ________________________ are persons saved by grace through faith in Jesus Christ.

7. Christians are ________________________ people in union with Christ.

8. Saved people have had their ________________________ forgiven, have been ________________________ by God on the basis of the atoning work of Christ, ________________________ to God, and ________________________ into the family of God.

9. Persons involved with the usher's ministry must strive to develop a sense of ________________________ and ________________________.

10. Ushers can serve as the eyes and ears for the ________________________, to let him know of situations that may require his attention.

11. Ushers must not allow themselves to crystallize into social groups or become ________________________ from the mainstream of church fellowship.

NOTES

CHAPTER EIGHT

The Usher and Ministry

Ministry is what we do when we reach out, through our service, to meet the needs of others. Though ministry can take many different forms, the ultimate goal should be to lead persons to Christ.

Ministry should be holistic in nature. In other words, we must seek to meet the needs of those we encounter on every level - emotionally, spiritually, physically, socially and mentally. Indeed, to be concerned with physical needs while neglecting the good news of Jesus Christ becomes a missed opportunity to lead someone to salvation. On the other hand, to tell someone about the love of Jesus when you know that the person needs a good meal becomes a missed opportunity to demonstrate the love of Jesus.

As we minister, we must also be inclusive. We must remember that Jesus Christ came for all people. Age, gender, race, social class and economic status do not matter with Jesus. No one is outside the scope of His love. Indeed, God desires to reconcile all people unto Himself. Thus, we do not have the right to pick and choose who we will minister to.

Lastly, we must be sincere in our ministry. To fail to be sincere is to misrepresent God. Thus, our ministry should grow out of genuine love, care and concern. It should grow out of our desire to see everyone receive the gift of salvation and the blessings which accompany the gift.

Ministry grows out of our service and service is central to Christian discipleship. Indeed, Jesus said, "Whosoever will be great among you, let that person be your servant" (Matthew 20:26). The Holy Spirit has uniquely equipped each Christian with spiritual gifts to be used in their service of God. Indeed, the Word of God tells us, "Now there are varieties of gifts, but the same Spirit, and there are varieties of service, but the same Lord; and there are varieties of activities, but it is the same God who activates all of them in everyone. To each is given the manifestation of the Spirit for the common good" (1 Corinthians 12:4-7). Thus, we see that every Christian has at least one spiritual gift, given by the Holy Spirit, which is to be used in our service of God.

> ***Every believer should be involved in ministry.***

As we use the gifts God has equipped us with to reach out to meet needs, we demonstrate God's love. We put the gospel into action. We become instruments to show a lost world the sacrificial, unconditional love of God. We truly become God's hands, eyes, ears, legs and feet. Through our ministry, God will be glorified. God becomes real to persons we come in contact with. Lives will be changed. Souls will be saved, and God's kingdom will grow.

Every believer should be involved in ministry. Indeed, it is impossible to be a faithful disciple of Jesus Christ without being involved in ministry. True ministry grows out of a life that has been transformed and renewed by the power and the presence of the Holy Spirit. To refuse to be involved in ministry is to refuse to be involved in God's work. Our involvement requires being intentional in our service and in our efforts to identify and develop our spiritual gifts.

The usher is in a unique position to minister to those who attend worship services and other church activities. Indeed, the usher may have an opportunity to minister before, during, or after a service.

Opportunities for ministry before worship begins include making sure Bibles, hymnals, visitors' cards, bulletins, offering plates and pew envelopes are in place. It may also be necessary to reserve seating for special guests. Thus, it is a good practice for ushers to arrive at least thirty minutes before the start of the service.

One opportunity to minister comes as the usher greets persons arriving at the church. The manner in which a person is greeted can really make a difference. Offer a warm smile or a friendly handshake. Listen to see if anyone has special concerns or needs. As persons take their seats, give them a bulletin. Find out the names of visitors and where they are from. In some churches, the usher has the responsibility of securing and giving the names of visitors to the minister so they can be recognized publicly. Notice when persons who attend regularly are absent and express how glad you are to see them when they return. Indeed, a warm greeting can really minister to a person's spirit and make that person feel at home, appreciated and loved.

The usher may also meet persons who are not familiar with the church facilities. These persons may need direction or they may need to be taken somewhere like the pastor's office or the choir room. This is especially true when another church is visiting. A warm smile, a courteous word, a friendly handshake or nod, or taking the time to escort the individual to their destination can really minister to that person, provide a practical demonstration of God's love and open the door for even greater sharing.

The usher may also meet persons who have special needs due to physical conditions such as hearing disabilities and an inability to negotiate steps. Persons with such needs sometimes feel uncomfortable or self-conscious. By being sensitive and caring, the usher can make sure such persons are comfortable physically, emotionally and socially.

The usher may also be called upon to minister to the needs of the pastor and other persons seated in the pulpit. Depending upon the protocol in a particular church, it may be the usher's responsibility to do the following: make sure there are glasses and water in the pulpit, make sure that persons sitting in the pulpit have bulletins and deliver messages to persons seated there.

Sometimes, the usher will be called upon to minister during emergency situations. For instance, there may be cases when a person in the congregation faints, must receive an emergency message, or "gets happy." During these times, the usher must be conscious of ministering to the individual as well as to the congregation as a whole. Care must be taken to meet the need at hand while also being sensitive to the fact that those gathered are in the midst of worship. Also, the usher's ability to minister during emergency situations can be greatly enhanced by mastering emergency techniques such as CPR and first aid. Remember, the apostle Paul urges us to make sure that "all things be done decently and in order" (1 Corinthians 14:40).

The usher's opportunity to minister does not end once the service is over. It can have a tremendous impact when the usher remembers where he/she seated visitors and goes to them after the service to fellowship for a moment and to see if any further assistance is needed or if further information is desired about the church or Christ. The usher can also help guide and control the flow of traffic out of the sanctuary. In some churches, the ushers may also be responsible for tidying up the sanctuary after worship, turning off sound equipment, closing and locking doors and taking lost items to the church office.

Apart from Sunday worship services, the usher receives a unique opportunity to minister during funerals. Funeral directors are the official ushers during a funeral. However, their work can be greatly enhanced by the presence of and assistance of local church ushers who are aware of and responsive to the special needs of the grieving. The usher can express his/her care, concern, sympathy and love through words of comfort and encouragement, body language and other supportive actions. Indeed, it is important to remember that the funeral service is not for the dead. It is for the living. The usher has a unique opportunity to demonstrate God's love during a time of great pain, hurt and need. Service rendered during this time can be instrumental in opening the doorway for leading unsaved family members and friends to Christ.

Like funerals, there will be occasions, such as anniversaries and weddings, where the usher will have an opportunity to minister to ushers from other churches. Visiting ushers will be unfamiliar with the facilities and the procedures used by the local usher board. Thus, it will be necessary for someone to show them around and to provide helpful instruction concerning procedures. Indeed, it is always wise to have local ushers on hand even when outside ushers will be serving. Remember, Romans 12:13 encourages us to "contribute to the needs of the saints, extend hospitality to strangers."

The usher has an opportunity and a responsibility to minister to the needs of those he/she encounters with love and impartiality.

Coupled with the need to be procedurally effective is the usher's responsibility to identify and develop his/her spiritual gifts. Indeed, this should be a regular area of focus and concern for the ushers' ministry. Every gift is important and needed in order to help the body be as effective as possible and in order to help God's kingdom grow. To refuse to use one's spiritual gift or gifts is to hinder kingdom growth. Identifying and developing spiritual gifts will help ushers perform their duties more effectively, as well as, lead to the development of other ministries.

In closing, our world is filled with persons who are hurting and in need. The usher has an opportunity and a responsibility to minister to the needs of those he/she encounters with love and impartiality. This is not optional. Rather, it is a direct commandment from God. Jesus said, "Verily I say unto you, in as much as ye have done it to the least of these my brothers, you have done it unto me" (Matthew 25:40).

The Usher and Ministry

1. ______________________is when we reach out to meet the needs of others.

2. A holistic ministry meets the needs of others on every level -

______________________ ______________________

______________________, ______________________, and

______________________.

3. Every Christian has at least one _____________ _____________, given by the Holy Spirit, which is to be used in our service of God.

4. True ministry grows out of a life that has been ______________________and ______________________ by the power and the presence of the ______________________.

5. The first opportunity that an usher has to minister is as he/she ______________________ persons at the door.

6. The usher may be called upon to meet visitors at the church that may not be familiar with the church ______________________, or meet persons with ______________________ needs due to physical conditions or disabilities.

7. The usher's ability to ministry during emergency situations can be greatly enhanced by having mastered techniques of ______________________ and ______________________.

8. Funeral ______________________ are the official ushers during a funeral.

9. An usher's service rendered during a funeral can be instrumental in leading unsaved family members and friends to ______________________.

10. The usher has the responsibility of ______________________ and ______________________ his/her spiritual gifts.

11. The direct commandment from God, found in ______________________, commands ushers to minister to the needs of those he/she encounters with ______________________ and ______________________.

NOTES

CHAPTER NINE

The Usher and Stewardship

One of the most visible acts of service rendered by the usher is during the worship service while aiding in the lifting of the offering. In many churches, ushers participate by either passing the offering plate down the aisles where worshippers are seated, or by leading the worshippers down the aisles to the table receptacle into which the offering is deposited. It is of extreme importance to have a well thought out plan for the movement of the congregation or the passing of the offering plate so that the offertory adds dignity and not confusion to the service of worship. Which ever plan is used, the head usher and the worship leader should have communicated that prior to the beginning of the service.

However, as we have already established in our introduction, the focus of *The Great Commission Usher* is not centered solely on the mechanics of the usher's job. Therefore, it is important to remember that collecting the offering has a deeper meaning than just collecting money. It is symbolic of the worshipper's commitment and dedication to God as well as the sacrificial offering of self back to God. When the ushers carry out the tasks of collecting the offering in a uniform, prayerful and gracious stance, it can really add to the significance of the moment. In this way, our offering can really be pleasing to God.

The usher has an obligation to "walk worthy of the calling" to which he/she has responded.

The usher has an obligation to "walk worthy of the calling" to which he/she has responded. Thus, ushers should not be passive participants in the act of gathering the offering of the worshippers. Rather, the usher should be an active participant in the worship of God through the presentation of our tithes and offerings. This begins with an understanding of what the Bible teaches about the Christian as a steward.

It is a well established fact that money is an important ingredient in helping the church accomplish its mission. Money has been a tool used in our local churches to support those local ministries so necessary to our mission. As the usher carries out his/her duties as

...the usher should be an active participant in the worship of God through the presentation of our tithes and offerings.

"doorkeepers in the house of our God," they must always be mindful that the very "door" that he or she feels called to "keep" must occasionally be painted, or the hinges oiled, thus impacting the finances of the church in some way. Therefore, those who care about their church must at some point give attention to how to adequately provide for the financial needs of the local congregation which they are a part of. This financial reality finds many churches on the horns of a great dilemma. That dilemma is encountered as they seek to answer the following question, "What shall be the focus of our efforts to secure the money the church needs to do ministry and meet its obligations?" In other words, "Where are we going to get the money?"

It may come as a surprise to some but, the fact is that nowhere in scripture do we find instructions given to the church to go out and raise money. Rather, the New Testament program for the church is to develop "stewards." For those serving in traditional black churches this may prove to be a shocking and revolutionary discovery that may find itself in conflict with how "we have always done things."

Usher boards have often viewed the sponsoring of various activities designed to raise money for various projects deemed necessary for the benefit of the church as part of their reason for existing. These activities may range from the selling of dinners, sponsorship of trips and outings, or more popularly, the Ushers' Anniversary. Although these functions may have, and in some cases are continuing to be done with some measure of success in many churches, the question we must raise is how do these activities compare when lined up against the standard of God's Word? A serious study of what the Bible teaches regarding the matter of the Christian and his/her money reveals that the focus of our efforts ought to be on developing within the life of the believer, in this case the usher, a commitment to the biblical principle of stewardship.

The biblical concept regarding Christian giving can be summed up as follows:

1. God is Creator and Owner of all things, including man.
   Genesis 1:1, Psalm 24:1, Haggai 2:8, 1 Corinthians 6:19-20
2. Everything comes from God.

James 1:17

3. The Christian's first offering must be himself.
   Romans 12:1-2, 2 Corinthians 8:5
4. Every Christian must answer to God for his/her life.
   Luke 16:20, Romans 1:12, 1 Corinthians 4:12
5. Faithful Christian giving will be rewarded by God.
   Proverbs 3:9-10, Malachi 3:10, Matthew 25:21, 2 Corinthians 9:6
6. The grace of God causes Christians to do more than the law requires.
   *Matthew 5:47-48, Matthew 23:23, Romans 5:20-21; 6:13,
   1 Corinthians 15:9-10, 2 Corinthians 8:7-9*
7. A Christian gives his/her offering to God as a part of faith, love and worship.
   *Malachi 3:10, Luke 6:38, 1 Corinthians 16:2,
   2 Corinthians 8:1-4, 9:7*
8. Tithing is the plan of God for the Christian.
   Genesis 14:18-20, Leviticus 27:30, Hebrews 7:4-9
9. Because of the love of God, the Christian is compelled to give tithes and offerings.
   John 14:15, Romans 13:10, 2 Corinthians 5:14-15

The Usher and Stewardship

1. The plan for lifting the offering should add ______________________ and not ______________________ to the worship service.

2. The offering is the worshipper's sacrificial offering of ______________________ back to God.

3. The Bible does not instruct the church to go out and raise money, but to develop "______________________."

4. God is ______________________ and ______________________ of all things.

5. Everything comes from ______________________.

6. The Christian's first offering must be ______________________.

7. Faithful Christian giving will be rewarded by ______________________.

8. The ______________________ causes Christians to do more than the law requires.

9. A Christian gives offerings to God as part of ______________________ ______________________, and ______________________.

10. ______________________ is the plan of God for the Christian.

11. Because of the love of God, the Christian is compelled to give ______________________ and ______________________.

NOTES

CHAPTER TEN

Ushering Techniques

There are many ushering techniques. Two of the most familiar are: *The Wilson Method* compiled by Mrs. Gertrude Reed and Miss S. B. Wilson, published by the National Baptist Publishing Board and *The Universal Church Usher Method* compiled by George T. Grier and published by Greer Press.

The Wilson Method instructs ushers to stand in the aisle sideways with their hands down and crossed in front of them. The *Universal Church Usher Method* instructs ushers to stand in the aisle with their backs to the pulpit as to serve the parishioners, greeting and seating them. The usher in this position will have their right arm down to their side and their left arm in the small of their back with their left hand partially closed. In selecting the style most fitting for your church, your Pastor should be consulted and have the final say. Pastors should be able to display a sign in order to receive the attention of the usher who will then be dispatched to find out his/her concern.

Ushers should not move about when prayer, scripture reading, or special musical selections are being rendered. They should also not seat persons during this time. Ushers should also not serve in the aisles once the minister has given his/her text. However, the sanctuary doors should be guarded at all times.

Ushers work very closely with the congregation and Pastor. If the Pastor is going out to preach, and the church is invited to attend, the ushers should be on hand to serve. If there are any services going on at your church at the time the outing is scheduled, the ushers should always make sure sufficient ushers are available to serve at home before going to visit another church.

If a visiting minister attends your church and he/she arrives before the morning service and is known to your Pastor, you can escort him/her to the study. If they arrive after the "Call to Worship" you should seat them in the congregation. It is not the usher's responsibility to escort the minister to the pulpit before he/she is invited by the Pastor.

A trained usher makes a difference in a church. He/she displays Christian qualities, greets parishioners with a smile and is ready and alert at all times to make sure the parishioners are comfortable in God's house.

NOTES

CHAPTER ELEVEN

Establishing The Usher's Council

Many churches have more than one usher ministry in existence. This fact requires the coordination of these different groups to insure that the usher's ministry functions smoothly. One of the most effective means to facilitate this effort is through the establishment of the Usher's Council.

The Usher's Council usually consists of the heads of each usher's group or their designee. The establishment of an Usher's Council will enable the overall usher's ministry to do a better job of planning, coordinating, and evaluating the actions and activities of the usher's ministry.

There was once reported in a popular newspaper an article about a man by the name of Robert Manry. Wanting a new experience in life, Robert decided to attempt crossing the Atlantic Ocean in a thirteen-foot sailboat. This thirty-two-hundred-mile trip he completed in seventy-eight days. When interviewed by reporters about his greatest fears, re replied, "The risk of being run down by Atlantic shipping." He talked of constantly being afraid of having a collision with a vessel. He would deliberately try to stay out of the shipping lanes traveled by these ships. However, he soon discovered that those big ships would also stay out of these lanes for the same purpose. On more than one occasion he would look up to discover that he was on a collision course with a much larger ship.

This is a picture of what often happens in many churches. Different program organizations, officers, ministries and committees embark upon their own route only to discover themselves on a path of collision with some other ministry or program. The Usher's Council can be the means of avoiding unnecessary conflict and confusion.

The Benefits of the Usher's Council

The establishment of an Usher's Council will provide the church with several advantages:

- Helps to facilitate a spirit of unity as the different usher ministries work together for a common cause.

- Works to insure that the Usher's ministry remains on tract in doing its part in accomplishing the church's vision.
- Monitors the church calendar to ensure participation of ushers where needed.
- Facilitate the wise use of resources and avoids duplication of people, time, and financial resources.
- Seek to be "proactive" rather than "reactive" in addressing problems and setting goals.
- Enriches the fellowship of the church as ushers work with other ministries to promote purposeful, meaningful service.
- Helps the church to understand the Ministry of Ushering.
- Identifies ongoing training needs of those involved in the Usher's Ministry

Election and Term of Office

Persons become illegible to serve on the Usher's Council as a result of their election or appointment to one of the leadership positions in their respective usher organizations. They should remain on the Council as long as they hold their elected position.

Usher Council Officers

Members serving on the Usher's Council should elect their Usher Council Chairperson (referred to in some circles as the "In-Charge Usher"). The Usher's Council, under the leadership of the chairperson, strives to insure the cooperation of all who are involved in the Usher's Ministry and organization so that they may move more deliberately toward the achievement of the church's mission.

His or her duties include the following:

- Lead the Usher's Council in performing its purpose
- Prepares agenda for regularly scheduled meetings
- Notifies Usher Council members of the time and place of all meetings
- Presides during Ushers Council meetings
- Meets regularly with the Pastor for updates and input on how the ministry can be strengthened
- Leads the Usher's Ministry in identifying and developing a strategy to address training needs

Usher Council Secretary

The Usher Council Secretary may be elected or appointed. His or her duties include the following:

- Works with the Usher Council Chairperson in preparing the agenda for meeting times and places
- Records minutes of meetings

Director of Usher Training

The Director of Usher Training is responsible for the oversight of training of all who serve in the Usher's Ministry. The Director of Usher Training works with all Usher Ministries to insure that all new members and existing members in the ministry of ushering receive adequate orientation and training. They should work with the Pastor and Minister of Christian Education to insure the prescribed "Ushering With A Mission" curriculum is followed and being properly implemented.

The Training Director must be competent in and knowledgeable of all church procedures and signals. This individual must have leadership abilities and be a team player. They must be a person of considerable maturity and a problem-solver.

Head Usher Responsibilities

The head usher directs all ushers in the service. There must be a head usher designated for every occasion. This responsibility can be carried out by the chairperson or president of the usher ministry.

A Model of the Usher's Council

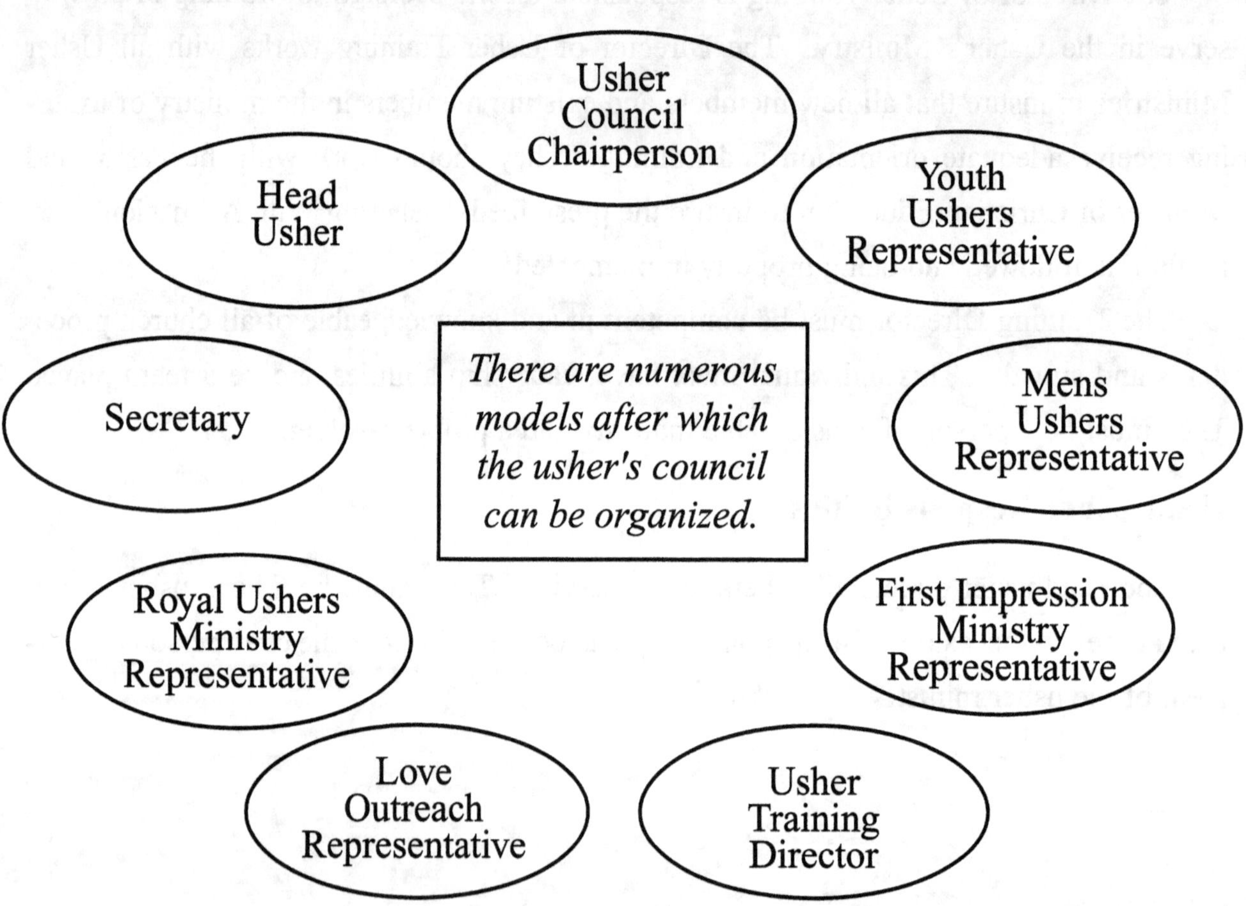

Your Church Model of the Usher's Council

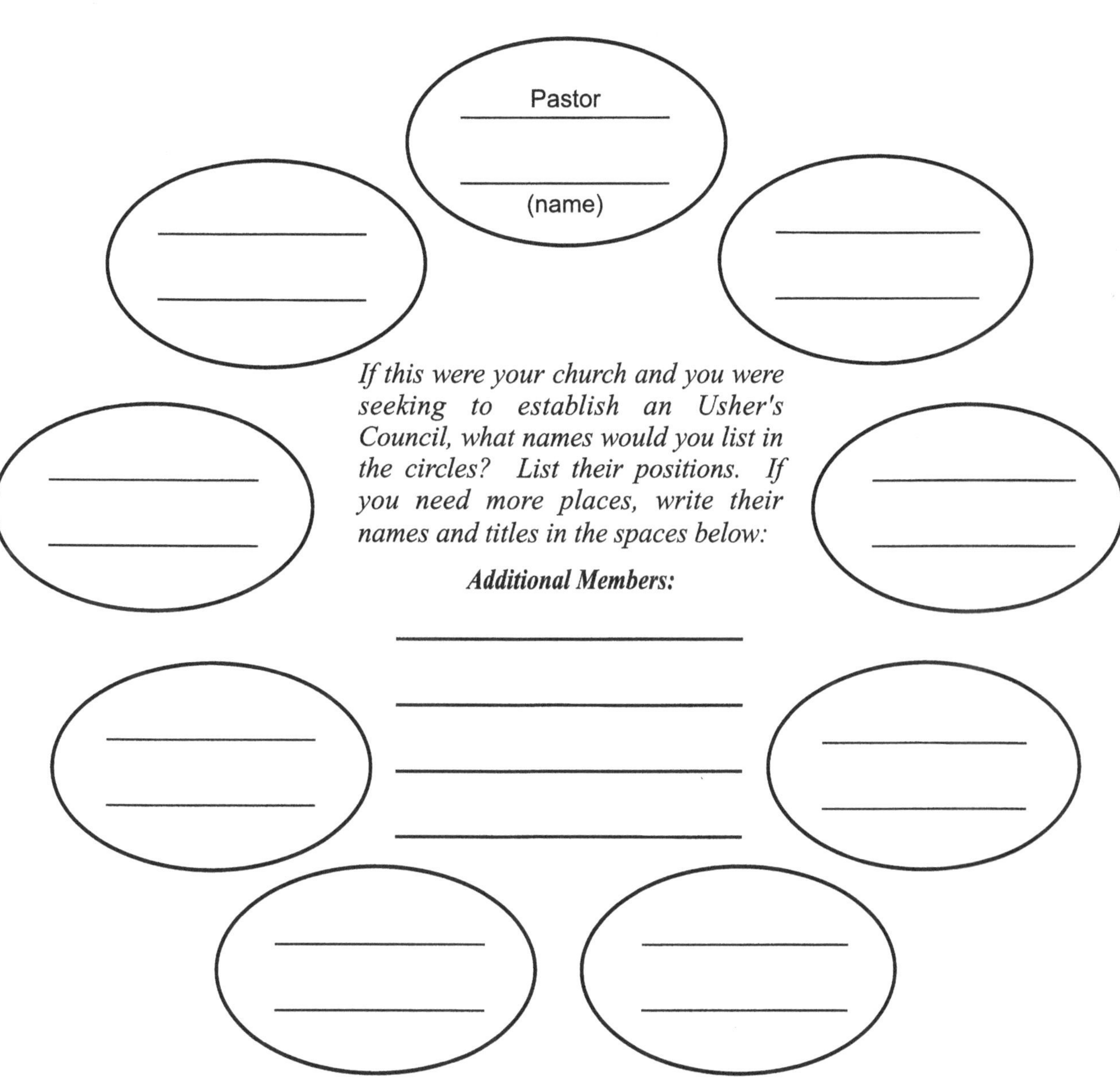

NOTES

CHAPTER TWELVE

Universal Rules and Signals to Use When Ushering

During the context of service in which ushers are serving, it is often necessary for ushers to communicate with each other using various hand signals. The following signals have been recognized by national ushers' organizations as universal.

There are also standard rules regarding dress and time of arrival. Though dress codes may vary from church to church, the standard rule shall apply when asked to serve at joint functions such as conventions or usher union functions.

Uniform or Attire

Ladies wear white dresses/suits, neutral stockings, black shoes, pearl earrings, small string of white pearls and ushers union badge.

Men wear dark suits, white shirts, dark ties, black/dark shoes and usher's union badge.

Time of Arrival

Please arrive 30 to 45 minutes prior to start of program (unless otherwise noted) to participate in prayer and receive instructions from the head usher.

Attention Signal

Place right hand on chest with thumb and first finger showing.

Service Position A

Usher should stand with right hand over left.

All Clear Position

Give the attention signal and then with right hand make okay sign (1st finger and thumb make circle with three fingers showing up).

Service Position B

Usher should stand with both hands down.

Other Signals (not illustrated)

Usher Change Signal The Head Usher will lead new ushers to each position and that usher will stand to the left of the position and remain there until all of the existing ushers have been placed; the Head Usher will lead them off the floor.

Leave The Floor Signal Head Usher will give the attention signal, then lift right hand directly to right side of face and make a downward stroke and then ushers can leave the floor.

Offertory Procedure Pass the collection plate with right hand and receive it with right hand.

NOTES

CHAPTER THIRTEEN

Implementing Ushering With A Mission

Ushering With A Mission is not a one-minute fix-all for all that may be lacking in your Ushers Ministry. Just as Jesus required a commitment from those who sought to be his disciples, becoming a "Great Commission Usher" will require a commitment on the part of those who are sensing a calling to greater service and a more fulfilling walk with God as they serve Him through the Ministry of Ushering.

Ushering With A Mission will require a commitment of time. Those who chose to embark upon this discipleship journey are required to complete the prescribed curriculum that will lead to the issuance of a Certificate of Completion from the national headquarters of *Ushering With A Mission* in Richmond, Virginia. All of the courses are designed to be completed in the local church setting. In some cases, some of the course requirements may be completed in the privacy of your own home. Some substitutions for recommended courses may be allowed so long as they fall within *Ushering With A Mission* guidelines.

Individuals desiring to receive credit toward Certification as a Great Commission Usher are asked to contact us by any one of the following means:

Website: www.ushertraining.com
E-mail: ushertraining@aol.com
Mailing Address:
Ushering With A Mission
P.O. Box 75121
Richmond, VA 23236

NOTES

CHAPTER FOURTEEN

Seven Steps To Becoming A Great Commission Usher

Step 1

- Conversion
- Memorize the Usher's Motto
- Memorize the Usher's Prayer used in your church
- Enroll in a Sunday School class
- Know the Biblical basis for the Usher's ministry
- Know the modern day history of ushering
- Know Universal Usher signals
- Take a spiritual gifts analysis

Step 2

- Take an evangelism class such as *Sharing Your Faith* or *Faith Evangelism*

Step 3

- Take a discipleship training course such as *Masterlife, In the Mind of Christ,* or *Experiencing God*

Step 4

- 150 on-duty hours
- Take a spiritual gifts analysis

Step 5

- Take a worship class such as *Prayerlife,* or *The Purpose Driven Life*

Step 6

- Take a stewardship class such as *Partners With God*
- Tithe regularly

Step 7

- Participate in an approved mission/outreach project

Upon completion of one or more of the required steps, a GCU course for must be filled out and mailed to GCU Headquarters in Richmond, Virginia. Certificates of completion will then be forwarded to the usher's church to be awarded to the usher.

Appendix

Portrait of an Effective Great Commission Usher

1. Understand that ushering is a ministry. Thus, the ultimate goal of the usher is to fulfill the Great Commission.
2. As a disciple of Jesus Christ, be committed to prayer and study of the Word. Thus, it is important for the usher to be a part of a Sunday School class, as well as a regular participant in Bible study.
3. Help members of the ushers' ministry grow and develop spiritually by including Bible study as a regular part of each ushers' meeting.
4. Know, understand and be able to articulate the biblical basis for ushering as a ministry.
5. Know, understand and be able to articulate the history of ushering.
6. Know, understand and be able to articulate your church's mission statement.
7. Recognize that each Christian has spiritual gifts to be used for the building up of the Body of Christ. Be willing to discover and develop your spiritual gifts.
8. Be knowledgeable about the following:
   a. Church facilities
   b. Church leadership
   c. Location of lost and found
9. Committed to the biblical principal of stewardship including tithing.
10. Able to handle emergencies and difficult situations with tact, grace and love while remaining calm.
11. Realize worship is an encounter with the living God. Thus, it is important for the usher to maintain a sense of worship and reverence while on duty.
12. Practice the techniques of ushering as needed.
13. Maintain a sense of fellowship by helping to nurture and support other ushers and by maintaining a sense of unity and team work with the Pastor and other ministries.
14. Look for and take advantage of opportunities to share the gospel with others.
15. Arrive at least thirty minutes prior to the beginning of service.
16. Notify the head usher if you are unable to serve as scheduled.

Purposeful Meetings

1. Keep Christ as the central focus of your Usher's Ministry.
2. Devise and set forth specific plans and procedures **(Always under the advice and guidance of the Pastor)**
3. Make Bible study part of every meeting.
4. Build community and fellowship.
5. Resolve any problems which might arise immediately.
6. Review assignments.
7. Meet monthly at a specified date and time.
8. Hold practice sessions related to:
   a. Receiving offerings
   b. Seating procedures
   c. Service position
   d. Prayer position
   e. Signal codes
   f. Procedures during different parts of the service such as:
      aa. scripture reading
      bb. prayer
      cc. sermon
      dd. offertory
9. Provide annual training workshops.

Checklist For Ushers

Item	Suggested Standard
Personal	
___ Dress or Suit	Clean and intact
___ Tie and Accessories	Neatly tied and in place
___ Shoes	Clean and polished
___ Shirt	Clean, neatly laundered
___ Hair	Clean, combed, well-trimmed
___ Nails	Clean, manicured
___ Badge	Always wear
___ Teeth	Clean, nothing in mouth, including gum or candy
___ Hearing	Keen
___ Voice	Clear and friendly
___ Flower, badge or nameplate	In place
Manner	
___ Friendly	Subdued, yet joyous
___ Helpful	Think from the worshippers viewpoint
___ Respectful	Know that all – young or old, rich or poor - are worthy of respect
___ Prayerful	God's leading and blessings are needed
___ Understanding	Alert to physical handicaps and needs of children
___ Thoughtful	Each person is a child of God. Remember name and seating preference.
___ Inconspicuous	Meet every need unostentatiously

Item	***Suggested Standard***
Sanctuary	
___ Clean	Sexton's job, but usher may help
___ Pew racks	Everything in place
___ Light	Adequate, not blinding
___ Air	Closely monitor temperature
___ Offering Plates	In proper place
___ Candles other appurtenances	Lighted. All accounted for
___ Church bulletins	Ready for distribution
Functions	
___ Greeting	People appreciate a warm welcome and friendly disposition
___ Seating	Only at indicated times. Give worshippers a bulletin as they enter the pews
___ Offering	In unison and according to plan
___ Tending	Awareness of all possible emergencies and knowledge of how to meet them
___ Worshipping	The usher is a participant in the worship
___ Waiting	Before and after the service
___ Promoting	Encouraging quiet and spirit of worship throughout the building
___ Cooperating	Working in harmony with other ushers and ministries to complete a total task

Assignments

Place a similar assignment chart, like the one that follows, on designated board and give one to each usher, pastor, diaconate and minister of music. This helps to keep everyone informed about who is assigned to what duty station and responsibility; and help others to know who to call on when particular needs arise.

Assignment Chart

Names, addresses and telephone numbers of all ushers are on the back of this sheet.

	April	May	June
First Sunday	Floyd Blair, Head Sally Barnett Paul Nguyen Henry Nelson Alicia Martinez	Nancy Metz, Head Alicia Martinez Floyd Blair Fred Brinton Oliver James	Carlos Rio, Head John Rudolf Gus Hadley Cheryl Penza Donald Frey
Second Sunday	Floyd Blair, Head Fred Brinton Oliver James Carlos Rio Bruce Flint	Nancy Metz, Head Carlos Rio Bruce Flint John Rudolf Gus Hadley	Carlos Rio, Head Nancy Metz Milton Arcot Sally Barnett Paul Nguyen
Third Sunday	Floyd Blair, Head Nancy Metz John Rudolph Gus Hadley Cheryl Penza	Nancy Metz, Head Cheryl Penza Donald Frey Milton Arcot Sally Barnett	Carlos Rio, Head Henry Nelson Alicia Martinez Floyd Blair Fred Brinton
Fourth Sunday	Floyd Blair, Head Milton Arcot Sally Barnett Paul Nguyen Henry Nelson	Nancy Metz, Head Paul Nguyen Henry Nelson Alicia Martinez Floyd Blair	Carlos Rio, Head Oliver James Bruce Flint John Rudolf Gus Hadley
Fifth Sunday		Nancy Metz, Head Fred Brinton Oliver James Carlos Rio Bruce Flint	

Prayers for Ushers

Option 1

Bless O Lord, your servant, just as You blessed the son of Levi who ministered in Your Holy Temple. Grant me Your wisdom to minister in your house so that Your name shall be glorified. Through Jesus Christ our Lord. Amen

Option 2

May I, dear God in church today, fulfill assignments in a Christ-like manner. Make me efficient in what I do, efficient in what I say. Understanding how I feel about people helps me to understand the attitudes I have toward them. I am thy servant Lord, use me today, I pray. Amen

Option 3

Be with me Lord, as I greet in thy name. May thy spirit of wisdom and grace be upon me. As I gratefully serve in thy house of prayer. Amen

Option 4

O God, you have called me to be a helper in your church. I recognize that some order is needed if I am to be effective. As your steward, I need to make the best use of your gifts in ushering. To be a disciple is to be a learner; help me to take advantage of the learning opportunities that are mine.

Option 5

I want to be a responsible usher. I want to be a knowledgeable usher. I want to be sensitive to safety, and I want to be aware of procedures in our church, so I can be helpful in every way possible. I am only one usher- but I am one. Help me faithfully to fulfill the duties of this work. In Jesus' name. Amen (*Church Ushers*, p.59)

Ten Points To Memorize

1. Serve the Lord Jesus Christ first and foremost.
2. Your ministry is important.
3. Attend Sunday School and Bible study on a regular basis.
4. You are a part of the worshipping congregation.
5. Work quietly and confidently.
6. Be friendly and courteous.
7. Follow the wishes of the Pastor.
8. Notify the Head Usher/ Chairperson when you cannot serve.
9. Be on time.
10. Attend Ushers' meetings.

Answer Key

Chapter One
A Biblical Foundations for the Usher's Ministry

1. doorkeeper, wickedness
2. guards
3. disciples
4. deacons, ushers
5. A. salt B. city C. light, candlestick
6. God

Chapter Two
The Modern Day Usher's Movement

1. 1822
2. men (male)
3. women, 1929
4. crowd
5. Ambrose Clark, 1914
6. comfortable, spiritual

Chapter Three
The Great Commission Usher

1. Great Commission
2. worship, discipleship, evangelism, fellowship, ministry
3. spiritual gifts, talents
4. Great Commission Ushers, Ushering With A Mission

Chapter Four
The Usher and Worship

1. worship God
2. holy, magnificent presence
3. adoration, reverence
4. shouting, singing, weeping, dancing, prayer, preaching, reading the Word, sitting quietly
5. Psalm 100
6. acknowledge, respond
7. confess
8. prayer, Bible study
9. presence
10. traffic
11. alert, attentive, aware
12. A. prayer B. scripture reading C. singing D. offertory
13. pulpit

14. goodness
15. God-focused, God-centered

Chapter Five
The Usher and Discipleship

1. discipleship
2. Jesus
3. lifestyle
4. selection
5. association
6. consecration
7. trains and nurtures
8. mature
9. "fellow", "fishers"
10. discipleship
11. The Great Commission
12. follow me
13. prayer, Bible study, worship
14. grow, develop
15. priority, commitment, time
16. growing, master

Chapter Six
The Usher and Evangelism

1. Good News
2. witnessing, sharing
3. relationship
4. cleansed, redeemed
5. abundantly, share
6. evangelism
7. experiences
8. God
9. life
10. Christ

Chapter Seven
The Usher and Fellowship

1. fellowship
2. Christ
3. destroy, sickness, death
4. race, culture, status
5. Holy one, human being

6. saints
7. saved
8. sins, justified, reconciled, adopted
9. community, fellowship
10. pastor
11. isolated

Chapter Eight
The Usher and Ministry

1. ministry
2. emotionally, spiritually, physically, socially, mentally
3. spiritual gift
4. transformed, renewed, Holy Spirit
5. greets
6. facilities, special
7. CPR, first aid
8. directors
9. Christ
10. identifying, developing
11. Matthew 25:40, love, impartiality

Chapter Nine
The Usher and Stewardship

1. dignity, confusion
2. self
3. stewards
4. creator, owner
5. God
6. himself
7. God
8. grace of God
9. faith, love, worship
10. tithing
11. tithes and offerings

Recommended Resources

Bible Guide To Discipleship and Doctrine by Avery Willis, Jr. This doctrine-based Bible Study helps adults learn how to use the Bible to gain insights into 13 doctrines, to grow in basic Christian disciplines and to participate in biblical actions.

Experiencing God: Knowing and Doing The Will Of God by Henry Blackaby and Claude King. This 12-session, in depth Bible Study helps Christians discover God's Will and obediently follow it. Daily learning and devotional activities help participants develop an intimate relationship with God so they can hear when God is speaking. Also available for children and youth.

In The Mind of Christ by T.W. Hunt and Claude V. King. Based on Philippians 2:5-11, this in-depth resource teaches believers how to think the thoughts of Christ. Topics include freedom in Christ, becoming like Christ, Christ's lifestyle, the servant mind, living in the Spirit and the kingdom within.

Masterlife: Discipleship Training by Avery T. Willis, Jr. This course is designed to help believers become better disciples of Jesus Christ in a small group setting. This six-month, in-depth discipleship process for developing leaders trains persons to fulfill the Great Commission command to make disciples of all nations.

Survival Kit for New Christians by Ralph W. Neighbor, Jr. Guides the new Christian in developing new thoughts and habits while developing a regular pattern of quiet time, prayer, Bible study and scripture memorization.

The Disciple's Prayerlife: Walking In Fellowship With God by T.W. Hunt and Catherine Walker. This course helps adults learn to pray through personal experiences, basing their prayers on prayers in the Bible.

Learning To Share My Faith by Chuck Kelley. Equips adults to use the Roman Road witnessing plan to present the gospel effectively to lost persons, mark a New Testament for quick reference, analyze a person's evangelistic potential, cultivate prospects, overcome barriers to witnessing and follow through after professions of faith.

Partners With God: Bible Truths About Giving by Bobby Edlund and Terry Austin. Helps adults develop a biblical lifestyle that recognizes God as the source of all material blessings and their responsibilities as stewards of all they possess.

Discovering Your Spiritual Gifts Module designed to help adults identify their spiritual gifts and to use their gifts in service to the Lord.

Decision Time: Commitment Counseling by Leonard Sanderson and Arthur H. Criscoe. Decision Time's thirteen sessions train persons to counsel individuals making commitments in worship services, revivals, camps and crusades. Guides persons to counsel and follow up with those making decisions about salvation, assurance, baptism, church membership and Christian growth.

Wise Counsel: Skills for Lay Counseling by John W. Drakeford and Claude V. King. Trains lay persons to provide basic counseling for those they meet in day to day living. A basic 10-step counseling module leads participants to learn to listen, guide behavior changes and interact appropriately in relationships. Provides guidance for counseling families, youth, singles, seniors, the sick and the grieving.

Togatherings: Fellowship, Folks and Fun compiled by Don Mattingly and Lisa Wilson. This resource contains more than 70 ideas, games, themes and creative activities for building warm, inviting fellowship.

Ministry Gifts Inventory by Michael Miller. Designed to help persons define their strengths as they relate to ministry and service in the local church. Not an exhaustive analysis of spiritual gifts. Highlights areas of strength based on what persons feel motivates them spiritually and enables them to pinpoint areas of ministry where they feel gifted.

Living Your Christian Values by Ralph W. Neighbor, Jr. Guides adults in establishing a Christian value system and in applying biblical teachings to every area of life. Provides daily instruction for individuals and groups.

Growing Disciples In Families And Churches This quarterly publication helps leaders see discipleship in a fresh, new way. Each issue helps leaders discover how discipleship can impact the crucial needs faced by churches and communities. Produced for leaders of adults, youth, children and pre-schoolers.

Bibliography

Bonner, L. *The Usher's Handbook: A Ready Guide for Church Usher*. Nashville: Sunday School Publishing Board

Clark, Thomas L. *A Guide for the Church Usher.* Nashville: Broadman Press, 1984

Edward, Diane, ed. *Principles of Church Ushering.* New York: National Council of Church of Christ, 1951

Elford, Homer J.R. *A Guide to Church Ushering*. New York: Abington Press, 1961

Foshee, Howard B. *The Church Usher.* Nashville: Convention Press.

Garett, Willis O. *Church Usher's Manual.* Chicago: Fleming H. Revell Company, 1924

Gills, James P. *The Dynamics of Worship.* Tarpon Springs: Love Press, 1992

Grier, George T. *The Universal Church Usher's Manual.* Greer Press, 1960

Johnson, Alvin D. *The Work of the Usher*. Valley Forge: Judson Press, 1966

Johnson, Kenneth M. *Church Ushers*. New York: Pilgrim Press, 1982

Lang, Paul H.D. *Church Ushering.* Saint Louis: Concordia Publishing House, 1946

Mims, Gene. *Kingdom Principles For Church Growth.* Nashville: Convention Press, 1994

Nygaard, Norman E. and Miker, Virginia E. *A Hand-Book for Church Ushers*. Encino: Nygaard and Associates, 1955

Parrot, Leslie. *The Ushers Manual*. Grand Rapids: Zondervan Publishing House, 1970

Principle of Church Ushering: Church Ushers' Association of New York. New York: Church Ushers' Association, New York, 1957

Reed, Gertrude & Wilson S.B. compilers. *Wilson's Usher's Guide*. Nashville: The National Baptist Publishing Board, 1991

Usher's Ministry Guide, Baptist General Convention of Virginia, 1996

White, James F. *Introduction to Christian Worship.* Nashville: Abingdon Press, 1990

Contact Information

Website: www.ushertraining.com

E-mail: ushertraining@aol.com

Mailing Address:
Ushering With A Mission
P.O. Box 75121
Richmond, VA 23236

www.ingramcontent.com/pod-product-compliance
Lightning Source LLC
LaVergne TN
LVHW080924110826
845155LV00039B/202